Catherine de Hueck Doherty

SOUL OF MY SOUL

Reflections from a Life of Prayer

AVE MARIA PRESS NOTRE DAME, INDIANA 46556

Books by Catherine de Hueck Doherty
published by Ave Maria Press

POUSTINIA

SOBORNOST

FRAGMENTS OF MY LIFE

Library of Congress Catalog Card Number: 85-72271

International Standard Book Number: 0-87793-297-2 (Cloth)
0-87793-298-0 (Paper)

Cover and text design by Katherine A. Robinson

Printed and bound in the United States of America.

To my son, George de Hueck

CONTENTS

INTRODUCTION

Thousands of books have been written on prayer. I don't suppose God minds the books, but I think he wants you and me to *be* the book. He wants us to *be* the word. He wants us to reflect his face. It's as simple as that. How do we do it? We pray.

Prayer is so very simple. Many people think it is something esoteric, as if you could learn to pray only after having studied theology and spirituality and all the different methodologies of prayer, from St. Teresa of Avila to transcendental meditation. I think if Christ had wanted to talk to Ph.D.s, he would have found their equivalent in the society of his day. He didn't. He talked to Peter and John. He talked to illiterate people who didn't know how to read or write, and they absorbed his voice and understood his words because he spoke so simply.

If you want to know what prayer is like, listen to a child of two or three. When we address God in a child-like way, that's a prayer. When we fall in love with someone and begin slowly, shyly, reticently, to explore

7

each other's lives as lovers do, that's prayer. When we are husband and wife, having entered into the fullness of our love in the great sacrament of matrimony, and experience the tremendous silence of a unity that is both physical and spiritual, that silence is a prayer.

Loneliness can be prayer, for every man and woman, married or single, in every vocation, at some time, is lonely. When that terrible loneliness comes upon us, a cry wells up deep in our hearts like the cry of a mute person, and rises to God. That cry is prayer.

How can you define prayer, except by saying that it is love? It is love expressed in speech, and love expressed in silence. To put it another way, prayer is the meeting of two loves: the love of God and our love. That's all there is to prayer.

1

FALLING IN LOVE WITH GOD

Why should it be difficult to fall in love with God? In the Old Testament, Yahweh says, "Even if you have prostituted yourselves under every bush, come back to me, Israel," and "If your sins be red as scarlet, I shall make them whiter than snow." Yahweh is the bridegroom of Israel; she is his spouse. Christ speaks to us constantly about being the bridegroom. The psalms speak of him leaping over the hills to come to his beloved. The Song of Songs says, "He kissed me with the kiss of his mouth."

If all of this is true, why do we have to inquire about how to pray? Perhaps we are really asking how to love, because, after all, prayer is simply an expression of our love.

Our prayer today should be like this: "Lord, I love you for all those who love you not. Lord, I love you for those who love you not." We could repeat it over and over again.

In Zen Buddhism, one is supposed to sit in the lotus position and meditate until nothing at all is left in the mind: Forget about yesterday, today and tomorrow and concentrate on the present moment. But, it seems to me, Christianity has a better idea. For us, contemplation is the contemplation of a Person. We contemplate God as two lovers contemplate each other on park benches, and when they are alone. They hold hands and look deep into each other's eyes. For us, prayer is like a woman contemplating her husband after the marriage act. Both lie still and gaze upon each other in silence.

Silence can be the greatest expression of love. Such silence is deep, unfathomable, and endless; it partakes already of eternity. Such silence touches the face of God upon whom, without God's grace, man cannot gaze and live. This kind of silence embraces Christ, touches the face of the Father, and knows by experience the reality of the Holy Spirit.

At first such silence is tremulous, because it is difficult for us to rid ourselves of extraneous thoughts. But little by little the silence becomes very quiet, and the person, with hands extended or with no gestures at all, loses himself or herself slowly into God. Or, rather, God draws the person into himself until everything is totally still. Then we know that God is truly present. Because he is present, this silence becomes the moment when the kingdom of heaven is here among us. Such is the knowledge we receive in the darkness of unknowing, where God teaches us about himself.

Our prayer is simple. Many Far Eastern religions repeat one word over and over, and we do too. We repeat the name of our beloved: "Jesus, Jesus, Jesus." We call this prayer "of the presence of God." When we close the intellect's window and open the heart's door, when we go into the depths of silence, we return with the name of God upon our lips and in our heart. Now we go about the world repeating it, and in this way we become a prayer. A human being achieves great joy when he becomes a prayer. Wherever he goes, he radiates Christ.

Prayer will come when we fall in love with God. The way to fall in love with him is on our knees. Everything in us resists this falling in love. Who wants to fall in love with the Crucified One? Who wants to climb the hill of Golgotha, eternally present to all of us? Who wants to be crucified on the other side of Christ's cross, even though this is his wedding bed?

But if we fall in love with the Crucified One, we shall know something else as well. We shall know joy beyond all knowing. We shall have peace, the peace he promised. We shall be able to lift up all things before his face. We shall make up what is wanting in the sufferings of Christ, for the body of Christ still suffers. Are we ready?

If we reach this point, prayer will spring like a song from our heart. Love will uphold it. Once we fall in love with God, we will love — even if we don't necessarily like — the untrustworthy, the ugly, the tired, the sick, the drug addict, the murderer, everyone. When we fall in love with God, we will receive the gift of compassion and of tenderness, for God himself is compassion and tenderness. With these gifts, we will really begin to be people of the towel and water, washing the feet of everyone, because now we know that everyone is Christ and Christ is in everyone.

"I arise in the night and I seek my beloved," says the Song of Songs. Suddenly I encounter him! There he is; he is here, just here! Now everyone around me becomes my beloved. Now it is easy for me to love. Now prayer comes forth from my heart as simply as a brook runs down to a river. Prayer is simply love gushing toward the beloved.

PRAYER: I Prayed

I prayed to God for songs and laughter. He gave me tears instead. I prayed for life in valleys green, full of harvest rich. He led me through deserts arid and heights where snow alone could feel at home.

I prayed for sun, lots of dancing, and sparkling rivers to sail upon. He gave me night, quite dark, starless, and thirst to guide me through its wastes.

But now I know that I was foolish, for I have more than I prayed for.

I have the Son for bridegroom. The music of his voice is a valley green, and river sparkling on which I sail. My soul is dancing, dancing with endless joy in the dark night he shares with me.

2

A RISKY BUSINESS

In his wonderful book, *Beginning to Pray*, Archbishop Anthony Bloom writes, "The experience of prayer can only be known from the inside and is not to be dallied with." This is a very wise statement. In many books, one has the impression that we should all learn to pray because prayer is so interesting and so thrilling, that it is the discovery of a new world where one meets God and finds the way to spiritual life. That is true, but the implications of prayer are more far-reaching than that. Prayer is an adventure, but it is a dangerous one. We cannot enter into it without risk. As St. Paul says, "It is a fearful thing to fall into the hands of the living God."

At Madonna House, our experience with the poustinia,* and with the million and one questions people ask, has shown us that we can't speak of prayer as if it were some new fad everyone should try. Prayer must lead us to total surrender, or it will lead us nowhere except back to ourselves.

Poustinia is the Russian word for "desert" and signifies a room where one goes alone to fast and pray. See the book by that title published by Ave Maria Press, 1975.

It is this surrender that we fear so much, and this is why prayer is such a fearsome and dangerous thing. This is why following Christ is indeed a risky business. He calls us to enter a revolution — not like the fight for a cause, but one that is infinitely more powerful. This revolution takes place inside of us, for heaven is taken by violence to *oneself*. Prayer is part of this adventure. Do not fool yourself: Once you encounter God, you will no longer be the same person you were before.

Today, almost two thousand years after the birth of Christ, Christianity still does not live in our so-called Christian hearts. Why is that? Why is the world not turning to Christ? It is not doing so because Christians are not living the gospel. We Christians have not followed Christ. Somewhere along the road of life we have compromised, and we continue to compromise. Had we really followed Christ, there would be no communism. There would be no wars.

How do we go to God in prayer? The answer appears in the beginning of St. Matthew's gospel, where we read, "The Magi saw the long-expected star." First of all, they believed. Secondly, in spite of the risk, "they set out without delay." Thirdly, they found the king, and "when they arrived at the manger, they knelt, they worshipped, and they presented their gifts." They contemplated Christ and adored him.

PRAYER: The Price of Souls

Is this the price one must pay for souls
that have gone astray? Is this the coin of love
meted out, like drops of blood falling on stone
one by one, hot, red, each one brought forth in
labor and in pain?

If this be so, then for one soul, Beloved,
take all of me.

Forgive my tears, for I am weak. But for a
soul I'll stand here, a lamb, as meek as you.

3

HOLDING THE HAND OF GOD

When I think of prayer, the sentence that comes to me is this: Hold the hand of the Lord, and talk to him any time you wish.

There is not a time to pray and a time not to pray. To pray is to pray always. You hold the hand of God. Sometimes you talk to him and sometimes you don't, but you are with him all the time. That is what our basic approach to prayer must be.

People think you need to set aside lots of time to pray. "I need at least two or three hours a day," they tell me. I do not think so. We don't need to spend all our time at our "prayer"; we need to serve each other! Of course we need to pray, but we can pray in our heart, constantly and without ceasing. Always you can offer up prayer for others, and in doing so, you are in touch with the whole world in a very beautiful and wondrous way.

When a mother is busy with her children, an employee with his job, a missionary with the poor, they may think they have no time to pray. That isn't true.

You give your time to everyone and everything, but in your heart, you pray continuously. You know that the Lord is very near, and that he holds your hand, as it were, while you go about your business. That's the way you should pray.

Obviously, there are times specifically allotted for prayer. The Mass is the outstanding prayer for all Catholics. In the Mass, you find the Lord. He comes to you joyfully and gladly. Can you feel how glad he is to come to you? He is happy to have you there. It is very important that you be there, for the Mass is your rendezvous with God.

You don't really "pray the Mass"; you sort of experience it. The Mass encompasses you totally and absolutely. It is such a beautiful time. In some profound sense, you become the Mass. Do you ever think about it that way?

Between two Masses — the Mass of today and the Mass of tomorrow — you spend your time talking lovingly to God. There is the prayer of the Liturgy of the Hours in the morning and evening. One can always "take time" to pray before the Blessed Sacrament, or in the privacy of one's room. One can make days of poustinia. But the real prayer is simply the communication that constantly passes between you and the Lord. Prayer is conversation with him. You don't need to understand how you talk to God. You just do it. He loves to listen to you and he especcially delights in your silence when you listen to him.

God likes our prayer to be simple. All we really have to do is to say to him, "So-and-so is sick. Please do something for him." I think God would probably be relieved to hear such a prayer; how tired he must get of all our long-windedness!

Suppose you are traveling. From the window of your car you spot someone in a wheelchair. Put your heart in his hand, so to speak, and say, "Lord, help that person." In this way, you can pray for many people and many needs. Prayer should be primarily for others. God will see to it that your own needs are met. We shouldn't always be pleading, "God, do this for *me*, do that for *me*." When we say, "God, look after this person," he takes care of us as well.

With so many people to pray for, long prayers are not necessary. That is why I simply say, "Lord, take care of so-and-so." If you say that every day, and keep close to God, you will find that he remains close to you.

I wish I could take each one of you by the hand and say, "Come with me. Let's all hold the hand of our Lord and pray in this simple way." Few people think of prayer in this fashion, however. Most of us are not used to praying as life flows along. We are used to spending so many hours in prayer. We are used to "taking time" for prayer, when, in truth, we should be praying all the time. Prayer never stops. It is such a beautiful thing to hold God's hand and to pray always.

PRAYER: O Jesus

O Jesus, I want you to be loved by all, passionately, especially by Christians.

You are so beautiful. You are the Lord. Give us the grace to love you and make you loved by all we meet.

4

ON BECOMING A PRAYER

People ask me how I pray. It is always hard to answer such questions, but I do my best because I know that "prayer is a hunger," in the words of Father Edward Farrell, and my brothers and sisters are as hungry for it as I am.

I fell in love with God when I was six. This may seem like an exaggeration, but it isn't. God was close to me in the same way that a child is close to another child. Since I have a vivid imagination, God and I did a lot of things together. We even played ball! As I grew up, I wanted to share my food with him, until, somehow or other, I found out I couldn't.

I proceeded slowly, even painstakingly, to vocal prayers. Suddenly those were left behind, and I found myself in a new land — the land of meditation. I always compare it to going to a dance and finding a boyfriend who deeply attracts you. You remember and savor every word he says. My lover was Christ, and so I read the gospel avidly, meditating on each word. The gospel became my favorite prayer.

But the land of meditation was also a temporary one. Meditation fell away as old clothes, and now I was clad in the beautiful garments of contemplation. Life was entirely different now. It seemed as if the Lord himself were explaining things to me. In meditation, my intellect had sought the answers. Now God himself clarified this or that passage. I was lost in God in those days.

Where does one go after being "lost in God"? The answer is a strange one, difficult to understand. You will not be able to understand it with your head, only with your heart. What happened now was that I myself became a prayer.

A person who is a prayer is someone deeply in love with the Word. He is deeply in love with a Person. When you are in love with God, your head is plunged into your heart. It is the happiest time of your life. Of course, we use our minds as far as practical needs are concerned. The house gets cleaned. The duty of the moment is always there. Far from interfering with your life, "being a prayer" makes you very meticulous about doing little things well for the love of God. The detached, critical part of your brain that endlessly dissects and analyzes and reasons about matters of faith has gone into your heart. This is what it means to become a prayer.

Prayer is suffering. It is com-passion. Suddenly, out of nowhere, the suffering of humanity will fill you and you are like one dead. You listen to the news, and you are the man who has been kidnapped by terrorists. You become the woman dying of cancer. The pain of the whole world is upon you. At this moment, you don't "pray." You simply share the suffering. That is what it means to be a prayer.

From another corner of the earth, you hear good news! You hear of a fiesta being celebrated, and you share the happiness! Suddenly you feel like dancing in the middle of the night. You feel that perhaps God is dancing with you. Yes, you are becoming a prayer.

Sometimes you are empty. You look at yourself and say, "What am I doing here?" You feel as if you are no good. Temptations assail you, and a thousand tongues of doubt lick you like flames. That is when you become a prayer for the doubtful.

Sometimes you go into the depths of hell, a man-made hell, an atheistic hell. You identify with the atheists of the world. But you descended there of your own free will, out of love. Your identification is a prayer.

Prayer is a movement, an impetus of the heart. Three quarters of your life, you will feel as if you cannot pray. Of course, you cannot pray as you think you want to pray! Who do you think you are, an angel who can say to God for all eternity, "Glory, glory, glory"? It is impossible to pray the way you think you should pray.

Prayer is being constantly in the presence of God. You are led to it. The experience of the poustinia will lead you there faster. Suddenly, you know he is always there! You can't pray? He sits there and doesn't mind at all. He prays for you (Rom 8, 26). As you pray about the living, the suffering, the doubting, and all manner of things, God is there. Once he is there, all things are there, and you become a prayer.

When you have become a prayer, you will be ready to be identified with Christ. No one has the strength to be so identified unless it is given to them by God, and God will give that strength to those who, clothing the gospel with their flesh, become a prayer before his face.

Here we begin to touch another mystery more incredible than anything we can understand. This is the mystery of the Incarnation. It is the mystery of ordinariness, of the commonplace, of the obvious. It is the mystery of love.

What is more ordinary than a baby born in a cave in Palestine, where many people lived in caves? What is more commonplace than to go into a cave like that when all the inns were full? It was the obvious thing to do.

We can follow Christ's Incarnation into our humanity step by step, and at each step, the mystery of the ordinary, the commonplace and the obvious will hit us like a sledgehammer. He has taken upon himself our life — ordinary, commonplace and obvious — and our mystery. But by incarnating himself in our flesh, he has made us more mysterious than we had been before his coming. He has divinized our ordinary, commonplace existence through his Incarnation.

The mystery of God becoming man and of our humanity "becoming God" meet in prayer: the prayer of the Son to the Father, and our prayer to our Brother. At this point, the mystery of being a prayer is more fully revealed. By his Incarnation, the God-man was able to pray to the Father, and by our divinization in Christ, we are able to pray through Jesus Christ to God the Father. God and human beings are thus united in prayer, joined in the one prayer which is Jesus Christ. In him, we, too, become a prayer.

What is the key to this stupendous mystery that we are? The key is the acceptance of the ordinary, the commonplace and the obvious, all of which, since the res-

urrection of the Lord Jesus, are radiant with the glory
of God.

Look at the sacraments. Take a simple thing like
baptism, so very commonplace in the Christian world:
A child. Water. Oil. Cotton. A priest. Godparents. All
very tangible, very obvious, and yet who has really
plumbed the depths of this immense sacrament? Who
has considered what it really means to be baptized into
the death and resurrection of Jesus Christ?

What is confirmation? Confirmation is the reality
of being possessed by the Spirit. We enter that reality as
baptized children of God. "I will send down on you the
one whom the Father has promised. Stay in the city until you are clothed with power from on high." Do you
realize what happened? He told the apostles of the
power with which they were going to be clothed, and
with which we too are clothed in the sacrament of confirmation.

This power was given not only to the apostles. It is
given to you and me. It deepens our mystery, for we are
men and women of glory and power, provided that we
understand the obvious and the commonplace.

The ability to understand the dimension of ordinariness in these boundless mysteries can be achieved
only by faith — faith, and our acceptance of Christ's law
of love. It is not enough to believe it in our minds and
confess it with our tongues. It must be incarnated! We
must clothe it with our flesh, preaching the gospel with
our very lives. Then and only then shall we be men and
women who have a key to our own mystery and God's.

In this way, we will become more fully a prayer,
for prayer is born when the mystery of God and the
mystery of man meet. This power and this glory are
given to us so that we might daily become more like

Christ, so that we daily become the way to the Father. This power and glory are given to us so that we might realize that we are brothers and sisters of Christ, and that we too have been sent to do the will of the Father and thus to lead all to him. The power and the mystery that is entrusted to us is given so that we might ultimately say, "I live, not I, but Christ lives in me."

That is our power. That is our glory. That is our mystery.

PRAYER: They Ask Me How I Pray

They often ask me how I pray. What can I tell them, Lord, who am myself your most unprofitable servant?

How could I tell that first I lay prostrated in the dust, the mud of all the roads you made me walk? Where are the words that could explain those lonely roads, their grey, dry dust, and black, black mud?

How could I tell how dark the days, how cold the nights upon these roads? How to explain that all I saw on all these endless roads everywhere were green, rough trees, and you stretched out upon them, dying?

Where are the words to tell that when you took me off those thousand lonely roads, and sent me forth into the haunts of men, I wept; for then I knew my poverty and theirs, and so I wept and wept for my sins and theirs, and for your unrequited love of us.

Perhaps you'll give me words today to tell what now I know, and I praise you for everything—the thousand roads, their black mud and grey, grey dust, their numbing pain, the gift of tears, the sight of poverty. But most of all, I praise you for every tree I saw, green and rough, and you dying on them of love for us.

5

THE SHEPHERD'S FLUTE

Have you ever heard a shepherd's flute in Scotland, or in Jerusalem? It is so haunting, so enticing, so irresistible that you have to follow the sound and see where it comes from.

The Good Shepherd's flute is constantly playing. Our faith is really an apostolate of music! We are listening to the Shepherd's flute, of which all music is but an echo. If we close our ears to that, life will be miserable indeed.

The story of Madonna House Apostolate is the story of music that is prayer. Everything that happens to us involves prayer. Ours is the story of two prayer words, "Fiat" and "Alleluia." To say "Fiat" is to say "yes" to God, and this yes is often painful.

We cannot live these words without constant prayer. It is inconceivable to think we can live them by ourselves, but this has always been humanity's greatest temptation. Throughout the ages, we have tried to build our Tower of Babel that we might reach up to heaven. Every day, every moment, we polish the same old apple, that we might become like God. Because of this strange tendency, so embedded in our fallen human nature, it is imperative that we, as Christians, hear and put into practice the words of Christ, "Without me, you can do nothing."

These words, spoken two thousand years ago, have still not penetrated our hearts. We are reluctant to accept them. "No!" we protest. "It isn't true! I can do a lot of things without you — just watch me! I can earn your approval, your grace, your salvation — you don't have to give me gifts all the time. I don't want to recognize you as the Creator of everything. I want to put in my own two cents worth!"

Now, we *can* contribute our own "two cents worth" and more, provided we realize that *nothing is possible without God*. Once we recognize this, we can give him a million dollars! As St. Paul says, we can make up what is wanting in the sufferings of Christ. We can "wait on God," which is a tremendous and beautiful thing. We can allow the idea of total dependence to permeate our life until, like sugar dissolved in boiling water, the two become indistinguishable.

Prayer is my total faith in God as my Creator. I am his image, his icon, and without him, I can do nothing. Prayer is my recognition of who I really am: a saved sinner, capable of breaking my friendship with God at any given moment, and likely even to revel in its breaking. When I recognize this, prayer becomes a basic necessity for my life.

There is a strange, inexplicable restlessness that we all have felt at one time or another. We have restless feet, restless hearts, hearts that are angry and disturbed, hearts that reject the other, hearts that seek but never find. Praise be to God if we still continue to search, but only too often we are satisfied with less than the real desire of our hearts.

What is it, fundamentally, that we all seek? Some think that union with another will lead us to union with God. Of course it's possible, if it is God's will for us to be married. But let us not fool ourselves that marriage will automatically lead us to God. No! Married people have to go through the same travail of the spirit, the same dispossession and death to self, as they would if they were single, a priest or a religious.

There is no shortcut to union with God, unless God himself provides it. Once in a while he does. Sometimes he literally pounces on a soul. St. Germaine, an uneducated shepherdess, was one example of this; Bernadette Soubirous was another. After all, God can work in any way he pleases! Normally, however, we have to walk the road to union with God. He is the only one who can quench our thirst and still our restlessness.

Prayer is the passionate desire of a human being to become one with God. It is the slow discovery that in order to reach this union, one must be dispossessed of one's very self. There is a deep mystery in all this, and I am not good at probing mysteries. I wait for God to explain them, if he so wishes, or else I accept them without explanation. Patience is the key word here.

So there is this passionate desire for union with God, and day after day, hour after hour, we come to realize the price of that union. The images of courtship and marriage in the Bible should have warned us of this, for love and marriage inevitably bring pain. We don't often think of it that way, but so it is. I fall in love with someone I didn't even know existed three months ago, and now I'm worried because he's driving to Chicago and it's raining, and I can't sleep for fear he might go too fast and skid and have an accident. Before I knew this fellow, I was peaceful, but the moment I entered into a love relationship with him, the pain began. I didn't even have to wait until I married him! Where there is love, there is pain.

Suppose you do get married. You are full of beautiful dreams. Then you become pregnant. You vomit every morning, you can't make dinner, you get disgusted with the whole situation. Of course, you're happy you are going to have a child, but today, you're downright miserable. Eventually,the child is born. For two years it screams and cries, and you wonder why you ever wished such a fate on yourself! You haven't got the money for a babysitter, so you can't go out with your husband. You're tied down and shut in and all you ever get for your efforts is "Mwah! Mwah!" You love the baby, but oh, how you wish he were in kindergarten. Then when he gets to kindergarten, you're worried sick about him crossing the street, or getting measles from the other kids. When he grows up, you worry about all the things that can happen to teenagers. Then you worry about him marrying, and then you worry about *his* children. Love is like that!

Where there is love, there is pain. But whatever our walk in life, this kind of pain is God's way of teaching us how to pray. Everything that happens to us spiritually, everything that causes us to grow, will bring us closer to God if we say yes. This is what spiritual growth means. It doesn't come from what we do, necessarily, from all our actions and good works. Sometimes it comes from simply sitting and seeing the shambles of what we tried to accomplish, from watching what was seemingly God's work go to pot. You can't do anything about it, but watch. This happened to me. I knew dimly then what I see more clearly today, that this was the moment when God really picked me up and said, "Now I am offering you the union you seek. The other side of my cross is empty. Come, be nailed upon it. This is our marriage bed."

All we can answer in response to that invitation is, "Help me, God! I don't have the courage to climb on this cross."

Now we begin to realize that prayer is twofold. Not only does God give us the grace to believe and to ask for help, but he also draws us to himself more surely than anything we could imagine. His own desire pulls us toward himself until the two desires meet. Our prayer and the desire of God come together in one brief moment of union, which only whets our desire for more. It is an insatiable taste of that which we seek, and it will give us the courage to say yes to the next devastating situation that comes along, the next steppingstone to union on the cross which he, the Carpenter, has fashioned for each one of us individually.

Prayer is that hunger for union which never lets go of us. It beats into our blood with the very beat of our hearts. It is a thirst that can be quenched by nothing except God. It is as if one's whole body is poised on tiptoe, our hands stretching upward as if to touch the cosmos. The act of praying, like the act of love, involves movement and effort. You don't pray like a robot any more than you make love like one! Prayer is movement, stretching, seeking, holding, finding only to seek again, as in the Song of Songs, "I opened to my beloved, but he had turned his back and gone."

Prayer is walking up to an abyss, looking down, and being unable to see the bottom, for there is none.

This is where faith comes in. You spend years balancing on the edge, almost jumping in, then retreating. Suddenly, at some given moment, the hunger becomes too great, and the thirst too flaming. You jump! You jump into the abyss, only to discover that there is no abyss, but only God and the depth of his love for you. For a moment you catch your breath in his arms. Then once again, because he loves you, he seems to elude you, so that again you might go forth to seek him.

Prayer is constant movement, and strangely enough, it is movement into oneself, where the Trinity dwells. That is why dispossession has to come from within, for the obstacles that separate us from God are never outside us. "What goes into the mouth does not make a man unclean; it is what comes out of the mouth that makes him unclean." Dispossession is like taking a broom to one's inner being to clear out everything that keeps us from being united to God. If I ask myself what paradise is, I think it must be that recognition of the Christ who has always dwelt within me. Death will be the breaking of the barrier between myself and the indwelling Trinity. Then I shall know that I was always united with God, that he was always with me.

However, I don't have to wait for death. I can have faith that God dwells within me now. I am not trying to reach some distant star. As it says in the book of Deuteronomy, "It is not in heaven that you need to wonder, 'Who will go up to heaven for us and bring it down to us, so that we may hear it and keep it?' Nor is it beyond the seas....No, the Word is very near to you, it is in your mouth and in your heart." What matters is that God is in me and that I follow the Shepherd's flute.

PRAYER: Closed Doors

I beat my soul against the closed doors of
human hearts until my soul was but a mess of
wounds. You took me to your cellars, Lord,
and precious wines you gave me there to drink.
It seemed to me that I was lying within the
circle of your arms, resting upon your heart.

You sang of turtledoves, and of love having
come to our land. And then you bade me rise
and go in search of souls. For this, you said, "I
gave you the choicest wine to drink. For this I
let you hear the living love that is the beating
of my heart."

So here I am, on fire, exiled from you and
our land. I cannot hear the turtledove, and all
is dark. Yet I know you send me into exile
because you love me. Then give me strength
not to glance back but to run with giant steps
forward, believing that the wind of your will
can carry me to the end of the earth.

I live, exist, have my being within the
soundless sound of God's voice. I am
encompassed, filled, and drowning in the sea of
music that is his voice. It seems that I myself
have become but an echo of all his songs.

A troubadour am I, who wanders without
zither or guitar, yet a troubadour forever
singing soundless songs to all who come within
hearing distance of my silent voice. How can I
live and echo this sea of music — and yet be
silent!

6

FIRE AND TEARS

I often meditate on holy cards. Yesterday I came across one that spoke of prayer as fire and tears. It seems to me that this is a very real part of prayer. When you ask yourself where prayer comes from, you will discover that it comes from the heart, the heart that is on fire, and full of tears.

If I really pray with fire and tears, I find that the two go together. The fire is the fire of God's love. The tears are tears of compunction, or of gratitude. They form a river within us. Tears are the only river on which fire can burn!

To discover this type of prayer, we must be willing to look deeply into ourselves. We will get nowhere by loitering on the surface. We must somehow reach that level of our heart where prayer and surrender go hand in hand.

The prayer of fire and tears takes place in silence. Like all things of the heart, it happens very quietly. We speak to God in our funny little way that must seem to him as awkward as baby talk, trying to tell him that we love him, that we are on fire with love for him, and that we weep in gratitude that he has come down to us.

God listens and listens. He listens to us as no one else could ever do. He listens with his whole being, because he loves us so.

Sometimes our prayer doesn't reach him. It falls short because it is not rooted in reality. God created reality; he really *is;* and the kind of prayer he desires from us is *real* prayer. We can beg him for this and that, but if our prayer is not grounded in truth, that is, in reality, he cannot hear it. Archbishop Bloom puts it well in his book *Beginning to Pray:* "The moment we try to be what we are not, there is nothing left to say or have; we become a fictitious personality, an unreal presence, and this unreal presence cannot be approached by God."

Truth is love. We pray, but we fail to love one another. We fail to love our neighbor. We don't even love ourselves. We don't love our enemies, and we certainly are not about to hand over our lives as martyrs— "Greater love hath no man than to give his life for his brethren," said Jesus. We talk and talk about these things but we don't do them, and so our prayers, though they may be wet with tears and blazing with fire, fall short of God as if blocked by a brick wall.

In order for our prayer to be rooted in love, we must be willing to face conflicts openly. I can think of many, many examples. In any department of Madonna House, when people are angry with each other, they have to come together and talk it out. They must be willing to say, "Look, I am angry. This is why, and this is what is really in my heart." They also have to be willing to take the consequences of such openness. Here it may be the other person shooting the truth back to them: "You're angry because you want attention and no one could possibly fill the need you have!" But in other circumstances, outside Madonna House, the consequences might be much more drastic, and then we are called to say what we have to say without fear. Being human, we may well be afraid. But we will speak the truth regardless. If we do, people will not only believe us, but believe in us.

Throughout our lives, we will have to face things squarely. We will have to do it with our husbands or wives, with our friends, with our co-workers. We will achieve nothing by trying to hide our anger. As long as we fail to confront situations as they are, acknowledging our fault when the fault is ours, or asking the other about it if he or she is in the wrong, there will be a world of confusion and lack of truth between us and God.

We can hurt each other terribly, consciously or unconsciously. Why else would God tell us to love our enemies? My worst enemy may not be the communist — it might be you. I might be your enemy. You might feel like strangling me at times. This is always going on. We are called to truth, and we are called to forgiveness, but we are also called to become the cross on which the other is crucified. We have to be honest about this.

"People who trust are the robbers of God's grace," reads another holy card. We have to trust each other, and we can't go around muttering in corners. Such muttering is like a knife in somebody's back, and it stops our prayer cold. It is terrible to be truthful, and it is even more terrible to be trusting. But that is what we are called to do. We trust because God himself trusts the untrustworthy. That is obvious, because he trusts you and me.

Prayer is composed of fire and tears, and this is what we bring to God. We bring him the fire of our love and the river of our tears, those shed in the light of gratitude, and those shed in the darkness of sorrow.

If we live in truth, our hearts will be at peace. Now our prayers, purified in the fire of truth, and cleansed by tears that wash away the debris within us, will truly rise like incense before the face of God. We will be living and praying as Christ himself lived and prayed.

PRAYER: Against Peace

Faith is old, and hope is dying,
Charity's cold, selling and buying.
Who wants peace and all its arts now?
Soon may it cease, lift up your hearts
now.

Ask for danger, ask for glory,
the fear and the fun,
and life like a story
in the wind and the sun.

Send us now a sudden waking,
a royal row, a thorough shaking.
For we must be sharply goaded,
our souls all rust with ink corroded.

Pray you, Lord, at end of writing,
send us a sword and a little fighting.
Send us danger, send us glory,
the fear and the fun,
and death like a story
in the wind and the sun.

7

THE SPIRIT OF PRAYER

"My Father and I will come and abide in you."
Few of us really comprehend the meaning of these
words of Christ. Besides our baptism, besides the food
of the Eucharist which sustains us along the way, besides the psychological assurance and the spiritual reality of forgiveness in the sacrament of reconciliation,
what exactly do these words mean to us?

Christ assures us that the Trinity dwells in us. To
the Eastern mind, this is the very essence of faith, and
of our life as Christians. It is the starting point, to be
returned to again and again, like a fountain of crystal
clear water.

We talk a lot about our feelings of inadequacy. We
doubt ourselves. We feel we'll never achieve anything.
Well, that's not too serious. But when we see ourselves
as worthless, filled with guilt, suffering from inferiority
complexes no psychiatrist could ever cure, how then
can we enter into ourselves and believe that God lives
within us? We have to shake that guilt from ourselves
like we shake out a rug. We have to get a broom and

sweep the cobwebs from our minds, for God has made his abode in us. His words are clear, precise and simple: "My Father and I will come and dwell in you." He doesn't say, "We will dwell in you if you are good." He simply says, "We will be there." God loves us, not because *we* are good, but because *he* is good.

The essence of life is the Trinity dwelling in me. The essence of life is the journey inward, deeper and deeper to the Source of all life. Whatever beautiful thoughts you may have, however much they may be inspired by the Holy Spirit, know that they are drops in a bucket, drawn from the infinite ocean of life within you.

God is movement, God is creation, and creation is always movement. God is fire, the fire of love. God is wind, the wind of the Holy Spirit coming down on the apostles. He is not a destructive wind, but one that cleanses us from the oppressive heat, one that picks us up and carries us from one place to another.

All this is symbolic, of course. We say that the Trinity is fire and wind and movement because "Trinity" is a concept that we can never understand with our minds. We can only enter into its mystery, into the heart of the flame, into the eye of the whirlwind, by the grace of the second person of the Trinity who is Jesus Christ.

Daily we enter the Trinity through our journey inward. There I find the God who dwells in my heart. Immediately, I open wide my arms to embrace my brother and sister with this renewed life! I touch God, I touch you, and I am cruciform as a Christian is meant to be. I pick you up and bring you with me, not into myself but upwards. I lift you up to the Trinity.

Tolstoy has a beautiful story about prayer to the

Trinity. It is the story of a Russian bishop who was making a visitation of his diocese. In that diocese was a forgotten island to which no one ever went. But when the bishop heard that three hermits dwelt there, he felt obliged to go see them — after all, they were under his care. Arriving at the island, he found three old men who kept repeating, "Three are thee and three are we have mercy on us." That was the only prayer they knew. "Are you hermits?" the bishop asked. "We don't know what that means," they replied. "We just came here to praise God by remembering that he is three and we are three."

Now the bishop was a little worried at this, and he set about teaching them the Lord's Prayer. They worked assiduously, and after a full day, the old men had finally managed to learn it. The bishop blessed them, and got into his boat, admonishing them to remember the prayer. When the boat was already quite a way out to sea, someone cried, "Look! What is that?" And lo, skimming along the water was a light, and as it approached, they saw the three old men gliding rapidly on the surface of the waves. Approaching the boat, the old men called out to the bishop, "Father, we have forgotten your prayer, so we came to learn it again — just tell us from there!" But the bishop crossed himself and said, "It is not for me to teach you. Your own prayer will reach the Lord. Pray for us sinners." He bowed low before the three hermits, and the holy men turned and went back across the sea. As they receded into the distance, their song could still be heard, "Three are thee, and three are we, have mercy on us."

So you see that there are times when it is better not to try to teach anyone to pray, even to pray the Our Father. God himself is the teacher. It is true that grace works on nature. But we are open to God's direct action as well, capable of knowing him by any means he desires.

For there is a moment when God calls you. It is as if he sounds a note, as on a tuning fork, and it reverberates in your heart. It might resound in the midst of a busy Harlem street, or in the depth of solitude, on a train or airplane, or on a crowded New York subway. But you hear it unmistakably. "Now!" it says. "Now! Arise and go. Go to this place or that. Go speak to this person or that one. Arise, go, write this book or article. Arise and be reconciled with your neighbor. Arise and take the step for which I have been preparing you."

At this point, you hold on to your chair, symbolically speaking. The last thing you want to do is to arise and go, because when God calls us, he purifies through suffering those whom he chooses. If you follow him, you may be spit upon, or have stones thrown at you. You may be called "white meat," as I was when I tried to speak about racial justice in the Deep South during the 1940s. But when you hear God's call, it is more agonizing to sit still than to obey. Such was the experience of Jonah, of Jeremiah, and of many other prophets.

There will be a tremendous turmoil in you. You will feel as if you are being ripped apart. This is the beginning of your journey inward, the moment of realization that the Holy Trinity dwells within you, as well as outside of you. It is the moment of prayer. Not of long prayers, not of prayer as you or I might understand it. Here I don't even mean the Eucharist. That is marvelous, of course, but there is something else, something so very simple. The moment when you hear God's call is a moment of recognition, a moment of receptivity and of deep openness. It is the moment when all we have to do is realize that we are creatures, and that it is God who calls us.

What is he calling us to? He is calling us to what each of us most deeply desires. He is calling us to a life that will bear fruit, for sterility is the most tragic thing that can happen to us. Remember the parable of the fig tree? God offers us fertility. He offers us a life of unimaginable fruitfulness, because he offers us the possibility of helping him build his kingdom. What is that kingdom? It is you and me, and the girl who takes drugs, and the alcoholic down the street. His kingdom is the lame and the blind, the lonely and the jobless, the rich and the poor. It includes all human races. It is the whole world.

We crave greatness for our lives, and God asks us to become little. To pass through the door that leads to his kingdom, we must go down on our knees. Paradoxically, if we do so, we will find ourselves growing in stature, for "eye has not seen and ear has not heard what God has reserved for those who love him."

This is a moment of choice. It is one of many such moments, for he will be called to choose every day of our lives until we die. But the fantastic thing about it is our freedom. We are utterly free to turn back from this power that draws us on. We are free to loose ourselves from the bonds of a love that demands our total surrender. Nothing prevents us from saying no. Nothing except God's love.

Thus, prayer becomes very simple. "Lord, I believe, help my unbelief. Jesus, help me." He is used to that prayer, and often it is not even voiced aloud. It's a cry of few words, a cry of agony, a cry for help, a wordless cry for clarity. But behind these short cries, accented with pain or sorrow, or sometimes even joy, lies the plea, "Help me to move on, to wherever you want to take me."

There exists a word that no one can really define, and that word is "faith." "Blessed are you who have not seen and yet have believed." The center of our faith is the Trinity, and faith grows as we journey inward toward the heart of the Trinity.

Sometimes it is very difficult to enter into this fire and movement and wind, and we become sluggish. We seem not to care. Prayer ceases to mean anything to us. The days become grey and routine, and we are tempted to say, "What does it all matter?" This is a type of suffering that is atonement, a plea for forgiveness, even the payment of a debt, if you want to put it that way. Such suffering is not devastating, but on the contrary, it liberates us. It is permitted by God so that we might advance higher up the mountain of faith. It is part of our prayer, part of the journey inward.

Prayer is contact with God, and in order to make that contact, we must begin to smash the idols that we worship within ourselves. Not until we begin the journey inward do we realize how numerous these idols are. We must take a sledgehammer to ourselves and smash them, one by one, in order to reach the fire and the wind and the movement of the Trinity. We tend to cling to these idols, afraid to recognize their existence in ourselves, and we worship them without fully realizing that we do so. But they must be smashed, for they are like stones tied to the kite of prayer so that not even the Holy Spirit can lift it.

To free our prayer, to cut away the stones that weigh it down, we must stop hiding our faces. Next, we must open wide our arms so that we are cruciform. Now we are revealed to others, exposed to their gaze. It is the beginning of that self-stripping that corresponds to Christ's, whose stripping began when he became incarnate as a child, and which gradually increased until his human body lay naked on the cross, a sign of his boundless love for us.

What is asked of us is that we go deeply into people's hearts. We cannot do this unless we are invited. We will not be invited unless we are willing to reveal ourselves to the other, saying, "Yes, I know the hell you're going through." Now there is a rapport between us. But to become naked in this way, to bare one's soul, is very, very hard. It is like opening the door to our innermost self, giving to someone the key that leads to the kingdom of God within us. This is a land without frontiers. I hand you the key to my heart and say, "Come in."

Are we ready to open ourselves in this way? Do we wish to love God and others totally, completely, defenselessly, without manipulation or the exercise of our own will, attentive to the tuning fork of God? Are we ready to pray the prayer of a creature called by God to a love affair with him?

God is love, and our faith is a love affair between God and humanity. "I believe, Lord, help my unbelief. Give me more faith so that I might bear the fruits of love, tenderness, peace, justice and truth, for the world and for myself. Lord, help me to grow in faith, which is the father of all these things."

Are we ready? Are we willing? If we are honest, we must answer, "Lord, I cannot do it without you. Teach me how to grow in faith. Teach me how to love. Teach me how to pray."

It is always hard to talk about prayer, because one is trying to express what is inexpressible. The reality is very simple, but words make it seem complicated. Nor can I talk to you about prayer in the abstract — I don't know what that means. I can only talk to you about the way I pray.

To me, prayer has always been a matter of listening. All my life, I have desired passionately to listen to God. When I was a little girl, I used to run in the low hills which were covered with wild flowers. My mother would say to me, "Where have you been?" and I would answer, "In the hills." "What were you doing?" she wanted to know. "I was listening to God." "How did you listen to him?" "Oh, it's very simple," I said. "You just lie down and the wind goes through the wild flowers, and they bend back and forth, and God speaks."

Of course, I was little then, and my imagination was vivid. But if you keep listening to God, one day you will see him, and this is what makes it an adventure. Now, I get up in the morning, and I begin to listen as I move through the day. As I do so, a tremendous peace comes upon me. I dictate letters, I sort donations, I look at books, I talk with members of the community and with visitors. Sometimes people are not feeling up to par, and there is anger and irritation, and the voices become a cacophony that rolls over me like thunder. But I smile and listen, and answers come because somewhere deep, deep within, I have peace, God's peace. In the midst of the turmoil around me, this inner listening brings peace. On a human level, I might be mad as a hatter at the things that are going on. But it is like a storm over an ocean; fifty fathoms down, everything is calm. Man is like that. The storm can rage, but as long as there is peace beneath it, all is well. It is a way of participating in the sufferings of

Christ. He too must have had some pretty stormy days, living with those twelve uneducated fishermen.

There is a tremendous joy in all this. Just think of it! At a given moment in time — for an instant — this Wind comes swooping down to take you into the inner heart of that fire we've been talking about. It doesn't burn you, doesn't scorch you. It is warm, tender, caressing, and you emerge from that fire cleansed. You forget about your inadequacies and weaknesses, because you know they don't matter to God. He doesn't care if you're not perfect. He simply wants you to come into that fire to love him, to merge your love with his, until you yourself become part of that fire, until everything is ignited by its sparks. "I have come to bring fire on the earth," he said, "and oh, how I wish it were blazing already!"

PRAYER: What Am I?

Am I a stone, O God, for you to write upon with fire? If so, O Uncreated One, give me the strength to bear your fire.

Am I plain desert sands upon which once again you burn a bush of fire? If so, O Uncreated One, give me the strength to bear your fire.

Am I a sea or mighty lake upon which you walk again with human feet that leave burning imprints? If so, O Uncreated One, give me the strength to bear your fire.

Am I a tiny square of earth beneath a cross, consumed and eaten up by drops of your precious blood falling from your fiery wounds? If so, O Uncreated One, give me the strength to bear your fire.

Do you desire all this fire you pour into my soul to light and warm someone? If so, tell me who. Or do you wish me to consume myself with love for you alone?

Speak, Lord, Beloved, speak. Or else your stone, your sand, your water, and your earth will die beneath the fire of your infinite desire. If so, O Uncreated One, give me the strength to bear your fire.

8

PRAYER AND DOING
THE WILL OF GOD

It terrifies me sometimes when I hear young people say, "God told me to do this or that, to go here or there." One girl who was visiting us said to me one day, "I didn't do the laundry because the Holy Spirit told me I should take a walk instead"! What is the theological premise for such a statement?

I seldom hear God speak to me at my own bidding, and in accordance with my own needs and desires. Under such circumstances, how can a person say with any real assurance that he or she is doing the will of God? It is easy to say, "I received all this in prayer," but unless it is checked by someone with a real knowledge of the spiritual life, such a statement will ring false.

I firmly believe that God inspires and draws people, but when he does, it invariably makes some kind of sense in terms of the circumstances surrounding that person's life. A woman once wrote to see if she could come and join us. She was absolutely convinced that she had a vocation to the lay apostolate. When she arrived, it turned out that she also had a husband and five children. It didn't take much to figure out God's will in that situation!

Today, young people want to make pilgrimages. I'm all for pilgrimages. My mother made pilgrimages. She loved them, and would readily walk 200 miles or more to visit a shrine or a holy place. But there was more involved than just the urge to get up and go somewhere. First, the children had to be cared for. Then, it had to be a time when my father was away and didn't need her. The household had to be in good order. It was only then that my mother went on pilgrimage. If any one of those conditions were lacking, she would not go.

This is how God normally works. He speaks to us, but what we hear must be checked out in relation to our responsibilities and our particular way of life.

I believe that God directs our lives. Of course he does! He directs them through the Ten Commandments, and especially through his great law of love. We are to love him with our whole heart, mind and soul, and our neighbor as ourself. "By this shall men know you are my disciples," he said, "that you love one another as I have loved you." He asks us to love our enemies and to lay down our lives for each other. If we do that, we are most certainly being directed by God.

The sanctity of St. Therese of Lisieux was such that she constantly obeyed even those who misdirected her. She found herself under the authority of a superior who was not very pleasant, but she obeyed to the letter. She even went to the pope for discernment about her vocation, and only then did she enter Carmel. There her sense of obedience to the rule was so great that when she was writing and the bell rang, she would lift her pen from the paper without even finishing the letter she was forming.

In the 1930s, I wanted to sell all I possessed, go to the poor, and live alone among them in a sort of "poustinia in the marketplace." When the idea came to me, I immediately checked it with a priest. I checked it with countless priests. They thought I was crazy. They all discouraged me, saying, "You have a son, and you are both mother and father to him." They told me that what I thought was an inspiration of the Holy Spirit was a temptation from the devil. One priest advised me to sprinkle holy water on my bed at night. I obeyed him. In fact, I drenched the bed so thoroughly that I had to sleep on the floor!

The discernment of all these holy priests turned out to be wrong, but I did my best to accept what they told me. In the end, however, I couldn't get away from the pressure of the Spirit. It became so great that I couldn't stand it. What did I do? My father had said to me, "If ever you are in a difficult situation, and you don't know which way to turn, go to the bishop. He is the father of your soul." So I went to Archbishop Neil McNeil of Toronto, and he allowed me to do what I had to do.

In this way, our Apostolate has existed from its very conception under the seal of obedience. To this day, I have never disobeyed a bishop or the church. A visiting bishop once said, "I've heard that Catherine has had many difficulties, but there is one thing she stands for unquestionably. She is obedient to the magisterium of the church." And that is absolutely true. I have been accused of every sin in the book, but no one has ever accused me of disobeying the church. Madonna House is founded on this obedience.

I cannot separate prayer and obedience. How can I pray to God, who was obedient unto death, if I myself act contrary to obedience? Christ my brother came to do the will of my Father, and I must do likewise. I must do so through pain, rejection and misunderstanding. Today God is raising up many people who honestly and sincerely desire to pray, and there is certainly much to pray for. But how can God listen to one who prays to do his or her own will? I cannot judge another, but on this point I stand before the Almighty in fear and trembling. As close as I feel to God, these are moments when I know he is terrible and awesome, and I prostrate myself before him, knowing I am nothing.

We tend to pray with great intensity for the things we want, but do we ever think of praying for what God wants? Usually, when our desire for something cools off, so does our prayer. It is very important, therefore, that when we pray, we move with the current of God's will, and not against it. This is true even when we are praying for someone we love tremendously.

When my husband Eddie was in a car accident and I was on my way to be with him, I prayed fervently that he might be well. But in my mind, every second, I forced myself to add, "If it be thy will." If God wanted to take Eddie home, for whatever reason, I had to be willing to accept it. I had to mentally pronounce words to the effect that I was ready to do God's will and to move in its stream.

The greatest act of a person is to do the will of God. You may ask me again, "How do I know his will? How do I know which ideas are mine, and which belong to God?" There is only one answer. To know his will, I must learn how to listen to him. This can happen only through prayer, and under the guidance of a spiritual director.

Try to think of listening as an essential part of prayer. You pray, and you hear the voice of God speaking to you very gently, not aloud, but deep in your heart. If you listen carefully, you will indeed begin to know his will for you. God wants us to do his will, and he gives himself to us continually, that we might follow in his footsteps.

Because you are in love with God, you can relate to him as you would relate to a friend. You can talk to him in order to find out what he thinks. You *want* to do as he suggests. Listen to him, then, that you may know. God speaks quietly, very quietly, but he does speak, and he will make known to you what he wants you to do.

You will do his will, and it will be beautiful. To do what God wants you to do is to be truly happy. Sometimes his will may appear to bring pain, but it will also bring you joy. Everything comes from God, and everything returns to him in our hearts. To give ourselves wholly to God, in prayer and in action, is the life of a Christian, and in it we discover joy so immense that our ordinary, everyday life is completely transformed. We find ourselves living in a new reality.

Listen that you might hear and understand what it is that God wishes of you. Listen to him quietly, and follow him. You will be filled with joy. You will also be filled with pain, but that makes no difference, for "your mourning will be turned to joy." This is what God wishes to share with us.

PRAYER: If We Surrender

How strange your ways, O Lord. On the brink of despair, you make love.

Help us to surrender to the duty of the moment, and there discover the great joy and beauty in it.

9

ANSWERING YOUTH'S HUNGER

There is a great sadness, but also an immense joy in me these days.

When I look around and see youth turning their faces toward God in meditation, prayer and fasting, I rejoice. I see them doing this in ever-increasing numbers. Around us in Combermere, some of the former so-called hippies, or flower children, have come to settle down on the land. They were among the most earnest of their generation, and it is amazing to see how dedicated they are to their ideals. They have survived the first winters, rugged ones with temperatures falling to $-20°$ and $-30°$ F. They chop their own wood, they fix up flimsy old farmhouses to make them weatherproof, and they bake their own bread. Even more exciting, however, is the fact that they fast and pray. These two arms of prayer and fasting have been lifted to God throughout the centuries, and the young people of today continue to do so.

Some of them talk of meditation and contemplation, of Zen Buddhism and Karma, Confucianism, Taoism and other Eastern religions. This is the cause of my sadness. It is good to turn one's face toward God, as long as the face is turned toward God. But, I say to myself, why don't we tell them how? For us Christians, prayer should be like breathing. The people of God have known meditation and contemplation since Old Testament times. Why are we not answering the cry of the young by teaching them these fundamental ways of reaching him?

One of my favorite descriptions of prayer comes from the book *Struggle With God* by Paul Evdokimov.

> "Pray without ceasing," insists St. Paul, for prayer is at the same time the source and most intimate form of our life. "When thou prayest, go into thy room and closing the door, pray to thy Father in secret." This means to enter into yourself and make a sanctuary there; the secret place is the human heart. The life of prayer, its intensity, its depth and its rhythm are a measure of our spiritual health and reveal ourselves to ourselves.
>
> "Rising long before daybreak, Jesus went out and departed into a desert place, and there he prayed." With the ascetics, "the desert" is interiorized, and signifies the concentration of a recollected and silent spirit. At this level, where man knows how to be silent, true prayer is found; here he is mysteriously visited.

"Here he is mysteriously visited." We are taught to pray by Christ, and the "Our Father" is the prayer he gave us. But when we are standing still and very silent, he visits us in yet another way. He comes to us himself, and the scriptures are opened to our understanding as if cracked by a nutcracker, the nutcracker of the Holy Spirit. The meaning of the words is released, and we are filled with joy and knowledge and awe. It is Christ himself who is teaching us.

Evdokimov continues:

> If one does not know how to give a place in his life to recollection and silence, it is impossible for him to arrive at a higher degree and to be able to pray in public places. The water that quenches thirst is distilled in the silence that offers us the indispensable withdrawal to view ourselves in the right perspective.
>
> Recollection opens our soul to heaven but also to other men. St. Seraphim says, "Acquire interior peace and a multitude of men will find their salvation near you." In this present time of verbal inflation that only aggravates loneliness, only the man of prayerful peace can still speak to others and show them the word become a face and a look become a presence. His silence will speak where no preaching can reach; his mystery will make others attentive to a revelation that has now become close and accessible to them. Even when he who knows silence speaks, he easily finds the unsullied freshness of every word. His answer to questions of life and death comes as the amen to his perpetual prayer.
>
> The essence of the state of prayer is to hear the voice of another, that of Christ, but likewise that of the person I meet, in whom Christ addresses me. His voice comes to me in every human voice; his face is multiple: it is that of the wayfarer to Emmaus, of Mary Magdalen's gardener, of my next door neigh-

bor. God became incarnate so that man might contemplate his face through every face. Perfect prayer seeks the presence of Christ and recognizes it in every human being. The unique image of Christ is the icon, but they are innumerable, and this means that every human face is also the icon of Christ. A prayerful attitude discovers it.

Prayer is such a simple thing. It has its own rhythm. You get in touch with God, and then you get in touch with yourself. Before I can love my neighbor, I have to love myself. Then I can love everyone else.

The young people talk about yoga. They talk about rhythmic breathing. There is a sort of intangible rhythm that is the rhythm of prayer. Picture this: A human being stands before God with his head bowed. His hands come together in a gesture of greeting, a gesture of prayer. He is embarking on that journey inward that every person must take if he or she is to meet the Triune God, Father, Son and Holy Spirit, who dwells in us.

Having bowed the upper part of his body, the man stands up again. Stretching out his arms, he discovers that he is cruciform. The tips of his fingers can now touch people, because he has touched God. This truly rhythmic movement of prayer is an important way of using one's body. Throughout the day, one should pray with the totality of one's self on the inner journey, penetrating deeper and deeper into the silence and solitude of one's inner being. Contact with God and human beings takes place on an ever deeper plane, for God is love, and our relationship is a love affair between God and us. Making contact with God inevitably must lead to making contact with others. In other words, prayer is for the service of people.

In the process, *kenosis* takes place. Kenosis is the Greek word for emptying ourselves in order that Christ might grow in us. What does that mean? It means that the dimensions of our heart must constantly increase. Because Christ became incarnate in humanity, we too can truly take humanity into our hearts. We can serve humanity in a thousand ways, including fasting and prayer.

Fasting and prayer can never be for oneself. They are always for the other. Modern youth, but not only youth, are seeking ways and means of emptying themselves of the self-centeredness and greed which permeate our North American culture. They want to empty themselves so that God might fill them, and so that "through him, with him, and in him," they might be of service to others.

Why, then, are we not giving them the answers? Why are we not preaching the glad news of Christ himself, so that people might recognize in us the features of the God we claim to worship and believe in? Why do they have to turn to non-Christian religions to find food for their souls and lives?

Some years ago, the bishop asked me to attend a theological conference in Toronto. One day, I was wandering around in the sunshine when I came across a group of hippies sitting on the grass at Toronto University, where the conference was being held. They had just been evicted from their residence, and people were bringing them sandwiches. One girl spotted my cross and asked if I were a nun. When I answered that I was not, that I was "a person," it started a whole discussion about Jesus Christ and how he was better than LSD! I spent ten days with that girl. I told her all about St. Teresa of Avila and St. John of the Cross, and all the

great mystics of the church. "Gee whiz," she kept saying, "They're better than Zen Buddhism!"

That was one of the most amazing things that has
happened to me. It was beautiful. The kids wanted me
to be their guru. "What about the generation gap?" I
asked. They assured me that with gurus, it makes no
difference!

Those were the years when the hippies started
coming to Madonna House. They were searching, they
were hungry for God. They fell in love with our Lady.
Many of them gave up drugs.

If that kind of thing could happen to me, at my
age, just imagine what could happen with younger
people, solid in their faith, going out to reflect the fact
of Christ and preach the gospel with their lives. It is
time we thought of that. It is time we stopped discus-
sing peripheral issues and plunged into the abyss of
faith which so few of us wish to enter. Yes, it is time,
and the time is now.

PRAYER: What Have You to Offer Me?

What have you to offer me,
in whose blood flows wild anarchy?

Are you the sun with potent fire
to infiltrate my slow desire?

Are you the wind to sweep my blood
gratuitously to such a flood?

10

FINDING CHRIST
IN MY BROTHER AND SISTER

I have a question. Perhaps I should say I have many questions, for who these days doesn't have a questioning heart and mind? But all my questions seem to converge into one: "How can I find Christ in my brother or sister, if I first do not know Christ personally?"

Like many of us in Madonna House, I read a lot. I read most of the current books and a large number of periodicals on all subjects and from many viewpoints — liberal, conservative, left wing, underground. From this constant reading, I see a definite trend emerging. In our day and age, with the revival of some degree of social consciousness, with the dawning realization of the state of minority peoples throughout the world and of the need for interracial justice, and with the growing recognition of the inequality that exists between rich and poor countries, Christians are finally realizing we must seek Christ in our brothers and sisters.

There seems to be some feeling that the personal approach to Christ through the sacraments and "old-fashioned" ways of prayer is now obsolete. With the emphasis on social justice, on the elimination of poverty, on improvement in personal relationships, more and more one hears and reads that the best way to encounter Christ is in and through another human being.

Here is where my question becomes acute: *How can I find Christ in my brother and sister, if I first do not know Christ personally?* It seems to me that I could not recognize him in my brother, had I not first met him in person.

What do I mean by this personal meeting? I mean the very essence of our faith. Christ gave us two commandments: to love God and to love our neighbor, in that order. But to love someone, I must know him. To know him, I must meet him. It is only when I meet and know him that I will recognize him among others.

How do I get to know Christ, so that I can love him and continue to love him in my brothers and sisters, and be able to love them because I love him?

The answer is that Christ knew me first. He knew me when I was baptized into his death and resurrection. Now he dwells in me and I know him when I undertake the journey inward into my own heart. I know him in the breaking of the bread. I know him when he "kisses me with the kiss of his mouth," when in repentance and sorrow I kneel at his feet in confession. I know him through the Holy Spirit who came to me, in his immense power, at confirmation, and who abides with me always.

I know him in prayer of all kinds. I know him especially in the great prayer of silence, the inner silence of my own heart. Breaking his own silence, he speaks when my heart ceases to be noisy, and I beg, "Lord, speak, your servant is listening."

True, I could learn much about God through books and techniques of the mind, but there is a vast difference between knowing *about* God and knowing God. Only those to whom he reveals himself know him.

This brings us back to prayer and the sacraments. It is in the sacraments that we make contact with God the Father, God the Son, and God the Holy Spirit. Through the sacraments, we come to know God directly, tangibly. Then and only then can we go forth to all humanity. Only then can we recognize his face in other people.

To me, this is the essence. Many of the ideas I read are on the periphery, like moths darting hither, thither and yon around a light. How can we love people if we do not love God first? Love of others is the fruit of our love for God. If the love of God is not there, why bother calling ourselves Christians? We are mere humanitarians.

PRAYER: Seeking

I seek you, Lord, so long, so passionately, without ceasing, but your mysteries close in on me.

For there is nothing easier than finding you. You are "they," my neighbor, everyone whom my eyes touch. You are bread, wine, served to me these days on platter golden at Mass. But your mysteries close in on me.

My eyes are held, beholding neighbor, and strangers passing by. Bread and wine on golden platter plunge me into faith darker than the darkest night. Yes, your mysteries close in on me.

Yet I go on, for I am driven by love that knows no end, to come to your dwelling among us, your children. Yet again, dark faith engulfs me, lifting me to unknown heights, or dashing me into immeasurable depths.

I seek you, Lord, so long, so passionately, without ceasing. Yet all I have found is darkness, depths, heights. These have led me to more hunger for you, Beloved. Behold me then, a pilgrim of love, appearing before your hidden face, my Lord, wrapped in your mysteries, with nothing but faith and loving hunger to pierce them with.

11

WITHOUT ME
YOU CAN DO NOTHING

"I am the light of the world," said Christ. Because he has come, we are no longer living in the shadow of death. We can live in light. But light is only light in contrast to darkness. Without darkness, we would not know the light. God allows us to enter the darkness because he desires intensely that we identify with him, who took on himself the darkness of sin. In the darkness, we experience our helplessness and powerlessness. In the darkness, we are blind. Now God can heal us. The act of faith takes place in darkness, in regions where intellect cannot penetrate.

When we enter this darkness of faith, eventually the light bursts in. But not right away. First God says, "If you believe in me, come. Walk on the water." The apostles were dumbfounded when they saw Jesus coming toward them on the water. Peter started toward him but began to sink because he lost faith. Most of us are too filled with fear even to start out. St. John said, "Perfect love casts out all fear," but we are so fearful that we cannot even imagine that kind of love.

There is a story of a child in a burning house. His father is outside, calling to him, "Jump! Jump!" "Daddy," the child cries, "I can't see you!" "That's okay," the father says, "I can see *you*." In our age we want to see where we are jumping. We want to see, not only the father, whose arms are stretched out to catch us, but the very earth beneath our feet. We want everything sorted out and in order. We are afraid to walk into what seems chaos to us. It is really perfect order, but we cannot see that. We want to say to God, "Let's get organized," and God refuses to organize himself to our standards. We cannot manipulate him — but oh, how we try!

Meanwhile the world cries out in agony. It cries out for salvation. Humanity may not know to whom it is praying, or whence help will come, but still it cries out. Jesus is the one who saves, and Christians are called to love mankind, and to assuage its pain. How can they help? How can they bring so many millions to true life? How can they bring justice and mercy to a twisted, needy world? Only by the power of God. Christ has said, "Without me, you can do nothing." But if we are one with him in prayer, we can do everything.

The real answer to our modern problems, whatever they may be, is to turn toward God with lifted hands, moved by love, trusting in God's promises and mercy. There is no other answer. If one stands in intercession with uplifted hands, as Moses did, then the miracle of God's action will take place. It seems strange, but the prostration of prayer, the dance of prayer, the rock-stillness of prayer, or whatever form prayer may take, floods the whole world with action. He who turns his face to God in prayer is in the eye of the hurricane, the eye of action.

Somehow, the miracle takes place. One remains on the mountain before God, but at the same time, by the power of his prayer, it is as if he walks the earth with his towel and his water. Prayer changes things.

When we pray, we have indeed accepted Christ's invitation. Not only did he say, "Without me, you can do nothing," but he went on to add, "If you remain in me, and my words remain in you, you may ask for what you will and you shall get it." We must lead each other to the top of the mountain to pray, because prayer is dynamic and prayer is holy. It is contact with God and union with him. As we grow in union with God, we come to know that prayer includes all righteousness, and from prayer stems all the goodness that God wants to bestow on humankind.

What is this prayer, what is this union with God? I cannot write a dissertation, but I can share impressions with you. Prayer moves a person's total being to communicate with the loving God, to respond to his great love. Prayer is this response that takes a thousand postures, from standing with arms uplifted in supplication to full prostration. Prayer is the fantastic movement of a dancer, and prayer is the stonelike stillness of a person utterly immobile, lost in regions that many desire to reach but which few really enter. Prayer is the bubbling brook of a child, or quivering words from the lips of old people. Prayer is the words of men, women and children who know God and easily talk to him. These words change into beautiful songs when they reach God.

People recite the rosary. They pray for all their relatives and all the needs of the world, vocally, simply, in a childlike way. Even when they sleep, their hearts watch for the Lord. When they pray, when they worship God, they are caught up in something greater than themselves, something that indeed is cosmic. The whole universe bows in adoration to God, and those who love him join in that adoration.

God is the only way. He is the only answer. And the only way to lead people to God is to teach them prayer, and to pray for them.

PRAYER: Black Fire

The quiet hush of your presence filled me.
But I was held in a dark misery, with bands
that tightened around my heart, in the cold,
dead, blackness as of night. And I was gouged
by a black fire that seared and burned without
heat, without light, but its penetrating light of
knowledge disclosed to me the ugliness of sin.

And knowing your beauty and infinite
perfection, I was filled with loathing steeped in
a weight of love pressing against the bands
around my heart.

O helpless Love. To see you hurt, to see
you bear, with infinite patience and such
forgiving tenderness, the careless
thoughtlessness, the cold ingratitude, the
noisome weight of sin, of my sins.

I had asked to bear your burden with you.
Was this your way of showing me the weight of
your cross, the pressure of the crown of thorns
around your head? Only the knowledge that
you could see my misery, that you could know
the limit of my strength, that you could ease
the burden of your love upon my heart,
sustained me.

12

PRAYER OF THE TOWEL
AND WATER

God writes straight with crooked lines, and I remember the passage from scripture that says, "My ways are not your ways, and my thoughts are not your thoughts." What appears hopeless to us may be exceedingly hopeful to God. And there is much that appears hopeless.

We in the developed countries have sinned. Lost in our affluent society, we have given generously of our surplus, but scantily of our necessity. Because we have sinned against our brothers and sisters, we have sinned against ourselves. It is said that faith and hope will pass away, but charity will remain. But I wonder, will there be any charity left? What will we find, we who have hated our Negro brother, disliked our Indian sister, and often despised anyone different from ourselves?

We have sinned in not fulfilling the second commandment, which tells us to love our neighbor as ourselves. We haven't loved ourselves and, thus, we haven't been capable of loving our neighbor. We present-day Christians have sinned by not showing the face of

Christ to the world at large. The early Christians showed his face to such an extent that the pagans said of them, "See how they love one another."

Why, then, do I feel hopeful? I feel hopeful because the Lord has plowed a field, harrowed and seeded it. I feel hopeful because green shoots of prayer are rising from the hearts of people everywhere, not only in those dedicated to religious life, but in men and women of all vocations. People are praying in their hearts, and they are taking time to go to quiet places to reflect. They are being drawn inwardly toward him who poured himself out in the service of others.

I see quiet service being rendered by one person to another in great simplicity. It isn't a frantic thing, where people rush to the ghettos to become social workers, or leave their ministries to become psychologists. No, it is a quiet service, person to person, and that is what Christ desired. His life was spent in prayer and service, and so must ours be. We must not only love our neighbor; we must take the time to listen to her, to have a personal relationship with her. This is possible for everyone, wherever you live. In high-rise apartment buildings, in private homes and condominiums, you can reach out to your neighbors.

You seek community? The greatest and most fundamental community is the Trinity who dwells in your heart from the day of your baptism. I touch the Trinity within me. I extend one hand toward God and the other toward my brother and sister. This is community. If I don't reach out toward them, the hand outstretched toward the Trinity will fall limp, because God will not grasp it. God and humanity, humanity and God. I am now cruciform.

In his inimitable way, God continues to bring

forth this prayer from our hearts. In this prayer of love and service, all arrogance, enmity, desire to manipulate must disappear. Unless we love each other as Christ loved us, we can pray and read scripture all we want, but nothing will happen. At the core of our prayer, there must be love.

We must strive for hospitality of the heart. Without it, hospitality of the house is nothing. We must accept those who come to us just as they are, without judging them, and with deep respect. The traditional Russian greeting to the neighbor says, "My brother is my life, and my sister is my joy." When you meet your brother or sister, do not probe and do not ask questions. If you stand there like Christ, accepting the person as is into your heart, God will reveal what he wants you to know about that person.

This attitude of always and everywhere opening one's heart to the other requires spiritual warfare. We must fight against all that is not God within us. This is the *kenosis* I have talked about, the emptying of oneself in order to be filled with God. This is true poverty. People are always asking questions about poverty, but it is very simple. When you touch God, you serve others, and you are crucified. What can you hold on to? Nothing. Not even your will. *That* is poverty! The things of God are so simple — *we* are complex.

When I am cruciform, I am free. I am holding on to nothing. Now I can be a carrier of the towel and water, wiping the feet of my brother and my sister. This, my friends, is the answer to all our social and political problems. This answer is based on my forgiveness and love of you, and your forgiveness and love of me. Until this takes place, we can expect nothing to happen.

PRAYER: O Lonely Christ
of Charing Cross

O lonely Christ of Charing Cross, Rue de la Paix, Boulevard Anspach, O lonely Christ of a thousand celebrated thoroughfares and foreign-sounding streets. Why is it that I have to meet you here, so far from home, when I have seen you lonely too in Harlem and Fifth Avenue? In Edmonton, Yukon, and Portland, Oregon, in Chicago, San Francisco, Kalamazoo, you were lonely too.

O lonely Christ of everywhere, why stand you there and here, so still, so sad, looking at the hurrying crowds pass you by — why?

Why are your eyes so full of hunger, longing, pity and compassion? Why do you lift your nail-torn hand and then let it fall again with so much sadness, as though you were a beggar about to beg, alas?

Why is it that I have to meet you across all continents, all celebrated thoroughfares, strange, dingy streets and palatial avenues, as well as wild and distant places?

Prayer of the Towel and Water

You answer nothing. You just look.

O Christ of Charing Cross, so lonely, you weep because the multitudes are hungry for your love and know it not. And because you hunger to be loved by these who know you not.

Give me the key, Beloved, so that I may open your loneliness and entering, share its weight. Behold my heart that you have wounded with love. Make it a door for all to come to you. Give me your voice and words of fire that I may show them *you*.

13

PRAYER AS EATING
THE WORD OF GOD

The Mass is the greatest of all love songs. It is our rendezvous with God, where he comes to us joyfully and gladly.

The imagery of the Song of Songs, and of the many scripture passages where God is spoken of as bridegroom or spouse, brings us to the very essence of prayer. Meditation, contemplation, songs of prayer, all lead to our union with God, not only in the hereafter but now. What has already begun through other kinds of prayer is now brought to fulfillment at Mass. God and humanity become one in a strange and incredible mystery that only a lover like God could conceive. The Mass is the incarnation of his immense love, and it is also the incarnation of our response: God and human beings are in communion. Perhaps at this moment, prayer as we understand it ceases, and the mystery of being possessed by God is revealed.

One day at Mass, the idea came to me that we eat the Word of God. I am always especially joyful when I go to communion, cognizant of the great mystery happening there. For me, the symbols of bread and wine dissolve and disappear into the reality of Christ's body and blood. I receive God in a mysterious way. The Mass has a tremendous power to unite me with him and all of humanity. He comes to me in order to be united with me. When I receive from the chalice, it is difficult for me to let go of it. The symbolism has vanished, and only the blood of Christ remains. I want to hold on to it as long as I can.

One particular day, as I waited in a state of anticipation for communion, I suddenly said to myself, "Catherine! Every day you feed yourself with the Word! The *word* can be eaten!"

In the scriptures an angel tells the prophet Ezekiel to eat the scroll on which were written the words he was to speak. This isn't exactly the kind of experience I am describing. It isn't so much that you swallow the word, but that the word penetrates you and fills you. You read the word of God at Mass, but it is more than reading. The word absorbs you.

The word of God is related to unity in a way so deep it cannot be expressed. It is related to *sobornost*, the Russian concept of total unanimity of heart, mind and soul that takes place in the Spirit.

It is as if the footsteps that Adam and Eve heard in the twilight move toward me, and I am absorbed by God, absorbed by the word. We read in the scriptures, "In the beginning was the word." All that God the Father created, he created through the word. It staggers my imagination to think that the word actually becomes one with me in this way, and I with it. I actually eat the word and become totally permeated by it. It becomes part of me. Depending on how completely I absorb it, I reflect it visibly, its rays emanating from me. I eat the word with a love and a passion that have no equal. Now the word fills me to overflowing. Now you see its reflection in me.

I become one with the word I eat so much so that I cease to exist. The word absorbs me in this way because I am willing, because I say to God, "Let me dissolve before my death. Let me be filled with you, so that every step I take is your step, and every gesture I make is your gesture." This is beyond abandonment, beyond *kenosis*, beyond anything I can describe. It is like the void in which one meets God. I have surrendered to the word. I have eaten it. *I am filled.* Now the word preaches through me.

From early childhood I have been imbued with the scriptures, and throughout my years in Madonna House, I have had a sense of this process going on within me. I was eating the word of God. He allowed himself to become absorbed in me. The more I absorbed him in the scriptures, the more he absorbed me. There was a tremendous mystery about it. Finally, one day at Mass, I was able to say, "Okay. I cease to exist. Now you are everything."

I'm still human, and I'm still living right on this earth. But I eat the word of God, and this gives me the strength to live and preach the scriptures. Most of my old fears and terrors have left me. I can say, "Now I live, not I, but Christ lives in me," for I eat the word every day.

We are all afraid, filled with feelings of doubt and rejection. I wish we could simply cry out to God, "Lord, you kiss me with the kiss of your mouth through the Eucharist and through the word. I eat your bread and drink your wine. You are the greatest physician, and I come to you directly, you who can heal us so quickly."

Now we can throw ourselves onto God. He is like an immense sea. He is like a cape that envelops you. He is a friend when everyone seems to have abandoned you. "Look, I am here," he says. "Give me your hand."

Now you realize that you have never really been rejected. No longer are your emotions churning and clouding your real love for those who have hurt you. You love because God loved you first.

The sea is warm and waiting. Listen to the waves calling you: "Come. I'll make you whole. Come. My waters will make you whole."

PRAYER: A Lover

Mighty, infinite, uncreated, why do you love us dwellers of earth? Why do I, insignificant earthling, feel the compelling, ecstatic whirlwind of your love?

Why do I know without knowing that I am alone in a crowd; that for you, crowds are all separated into brides and souls, and that for each one, you would die your thousand deaths in a few hours on a Friday afternoon?

All that is human in me dissolves at the thought. Like molten lava, it flows on itself and consumes all that it touches, which is myself. Then again, your breath, the wind of your love, touches the lava, and I am myself, a woman, an earthling again.

And again, the thought of your loving me, apart from the crowd, lifts me into heights that reduce me to nothing again. And again, a touch of your breath resurrects, and your love makes me whole.

How can I exist in this knowing that is an unknowing? How can I remain unconsumed while I am being consumed — a lover?

14

PRAYING IN THE NAME OF JESUS

When you are in love, only one person matters to you, and that is your beloved. The others are just a crowd of people. When our beloved is God, we must recognize that he is the king, and we must surrender to him. The self has to disappear. Prayer is this self-emptying. It means that we stand still and wait.

The Jesus Prayer might be enough for us. "Lord Jesus Christ, Son of the living God, have mercy on me, a sinner." Why would it be enough? Because it brings Jesus into your life. The repetition of the holy name brings the presence of the person, for in the Hebrew tradition, the name of a person is the person. Thus we read in the New Testament, "At the name of Jesus, every knee must bend." When I invoke the name of Jesus, I myself cease to exist. I am drawn into his name, immersed in his name, immersed in him.

Even in our secular society, a name is something very powerful. When I say the name Boris, for instance, I immediately think of my first husband. A person, a lifestyle, a whole period of my life becomes present. Certain names evoke particular events in our lives.

Some names suggest tremendous beauty, others evoke fear. Say the name of Adolph Hitler, and everyone shrinks, even the younger generation that barely knows about him. Say the name of Stalin, and you have a similar reaction. But when you say the name of Jesus, "it is accompanied by its immediate manifestation, for the name is a form of his presence," says Paul Evdokimov. Just say "Jesus," and whoosh, God is here! You brought him. I brought him. "Before the name of Jesus, every knee must bend." When you say "Jesus," many things begin to happen.

That is why cursing is so dangerous for the one who curses. Fortunately, most people in English-speaking countries have learned about Jesus at their mother's knee, and when they swear, they don't really mean what they say. When that name is really used as a curse, however, the curse falls on the head of the one who utters it.

When you say "Jesus," the word is already a prayer. You remind yourself, "If two or three are gathered in my name, I am in the midst of them." How much truer this is when we say, "Come, Lord Jesus," as we do in Advent. "Come, Lord Jesus." And he comes! This is reality, one of those strange mysteries that exist between God and humanity. We call and God abases himself and takes again the form of a servant.

Once you really understand what you are doing and begin to pray this prayer, it will continue even without you consciously willing it. Once you've called on the name of Jesus, his name will remain with you because you desire it to be there. He desires it to be there too, and the two desires merge into one.

Don't try too hard to concentrate. I might be reciting the Jesus Prayer even though my mind is on a hat I saw a few days ago. I can continue saying the Jesus Prayer with a hat on my mind. You don't have to get all upset, saying, "That damned hat! I wish it would go away! It's been interrupting my thinking and my prayer for days!" You needn't worry about things like that.

Russian Christians don't know anything about yoga, about mantras, about special breathing and all the prayers of the non-Christian East. Nor did the Greek monks. They prayed the Jesus Prayer naturally, and the Russians learned it from them. "Lord Jesus Christ, Son of the living God, have mercy on me, a sinner. Lord Jesus Christ, Son of the living God, have mercy on me, a sinner." In and out. In and out. You don't do it consciously; it just happens. This is the Jesus Prayer.

PRAYER: Lost in Your Immensity

Lord, I am lost in your immensity. I cannot find its frontiers. There is nothing to guide me anywhere, except, of course, you.

I am not lost as men would use the word, but I am lost in your immensity. I did not know your heart was so immense. I did not know it had no frontiers at all. Stupid of me, I know, for you embrace earth, spheres, constellations; all things that are beyond the ken of men are playthings for you.

I can see you playing with the stars just for the fun of it. Yes, I do. But as for me, I am lost. I try to tell haltingly, as little children talk, how you brought me to your void — yes, your void.

I thought and said that there one rests in peace. But I did not know that in your void — which is no void at all but an intensity of fire and of prayer — I did not know that the void was you, and that you brought me there to pray in me, so that I ceased to be, and you possessed me utterly, completely. So that is the void I talked about so innocently, so ignorantly.

Yes, I am lost, Lord, I am lost in the void of your love, and I am lost in your heart whose frontiers are beyond my ken or any human eye or mind or thought.

Yes, I am lost. But now I know at least one thing. I know that when I enter your void, I cease to be. They call it "all senses suspended" — at least the old writers do. But it's not true, not quite true, because the senses are not suspended, they are alerted, they are filled to the brim with you.

But then, why do you bring me into the void, into your void? Slowly, like a child learning to walk, I begin to understand, for in my hands outstretched toward you, you place your church. I did not know she was so heavy. I did not know she was so wounded. I did not know she was so torn — just like you.

I did not know she too was flagellated by human beings. That is another face of your bride, the face of infinite pain, as if the pain of all the world was gathered in your heart. Yet, so it must have been, for she is your bride, and the pain of all the world is always in your heart.

True, you died for the pain, you died for the sin that causes the pain most of the time; you died for all of it, to bring us back to Abba, your Father and mine. But as your Father said about his chosen people, we are stiff-necked, and so we did not listen. Perhaps we didn't hear at all, but most of us went about our business of silver and gold; and so the church was flagellated too, even as you.

And all this immense void you handed me. But who am I? You know only too well that I am a nonentity, a refugee, one who does not belong anywhere, and in a sense, perhaps, belongs everywhere, but not in a way that I can always feel. For I am human, God, and so I feel just like you did when you were human.

I am lost, Lord, but holding my hands forward, carrying the church, I don't know where to go, what to do! I am in your void, Lord. You had better guide me, or I shall perish under the weight of your bride.

15

THE GREAT POOL OF SILENCE

Prayer begins when one turns toward God. It could happen in childhood or at any point in life, when a person realizes who God is, and what prayer is. When it happens, the scriptures become a million love letters from God, to be savored, meditated upon, absorbed almost to the point where you become one with those eternal, fiery, gentle words. Reading scripture is like a conversation with God, a conversation which never stops, because every sentence moves the heart to greater love.

Praying the scriptures brings silence to our minds and hearts. Words in themselves can be terribly confusing unless one reads the word of God slowly and consistently. When you begin to read the scriptures in this way, they penetrate your being. You may not be able to quote chapter and verse, but the thoughts enter your heart. They become filled with light. You read the words and say, "Oh! That's exactly it! This is God's way of talking."

I myself have the childlike belief that God really

does speak to me in this way. When he speaks directly, it can be rather frightening and awesome, but when he speaks through the scriptures, it often seems less so.

Suppose you are thinking about something and are frightened. Opening the scriptures, you read that God said to the Jews, "Let us sit down and talk things over." Now this is precisely what we are doing with him when we read his word. Do you remember how God rebuked the Jewish people before he said this to them? He has reason to rebuke us too, but he invites us to sit down and talk, and suddenly things are different. When we realize we are speaking to God, our use of words changes.

Words are pregnant, pregnant with meaning. We don't think of them in this way, but so they are. They may be pregnant with good or pregnant with evil. They may be filled with God, the devil, or simply with ourselves. Here we must pay attention. When our words are filled with self, we are vulnerable to the devil, for we cannot be filled with thoughts of self and others at one and the same time.

God, of course, is The Other, and all others blend into him. When I pray, he always stands before me. I cannot get away from him. Because of the word, I leave all that I have to follow him. It is a fantastic thing. He became a man so as to take upon himself all other human beings, with their sins, their sorrows and their joys. He did so because he loved us. In God, I meet my brother and sister, who is my life.

Yes, words are pregnant with meaning, and I think it is for this reason that the church calls some of her sons and daughters to a life of silent prayer. In this holy silence, we learn discernment. In the great silence that takes hold of men and women as they grow more and more familiar with the written word, and with the

Word made flesh, all words find their true meaning.

In my book *Poustinia*, I shared some of my thoughts on the silence of the heart. I want now to speak more about this. A pure heart is a silent heart. It is a heart that watches carefully over its words. This doesn't mean that one doesn't speak. The silence is the silence of love. My heart is silent, and thus there is created an inner space where I weigh my words. The words that come at me from without also enter that silence and are evaluated there, not in accordance with my emotions, but in accordance with my love. Into this great pool of silence can be thrown all sorts of hurtful words, words that make me feel rejected and abandoned. The silence of love, coming from a pure heart, will examine with wisdom all that is said to me, and this love will determine my response.

It is like a laundry. The words that are thrown at me go through the cleansing process of love, faith, silence and hope. At this moment, what we call discernment becomes crystal clear, for it no longer comes from me but from God. It is God himself who reveals the meaning to me. Why didn't he reveal it to me directly? Because he wanted the words to pass through me first. He wanted me to accept the unjust things that were said, because this acceptance is my identification with him, and part of my own divinization.

Christ died to make me divine, and thus, I am a co-heir with him. To claim this inheritance, I must experience what he himself went through. Whenever impatience, complexity, or emotionalism take hold of me, twisting and turning the truth, as often happens when the devil gets his hand in things, then I can descend into the pool of silence where I think it over, pray about it and purify my heart and thoughts. This is the laundry of the Spirit, the purgatory of the Spirit here on earth.

When I enter this pool of silence, I become more charitable. Is there any limit to charity? The only limit is death. I die for the other out of love for him. This was the only limit that Christ himself knew.

In the pool of silence, I learn to be open. Openness is a door that never closes, a door that has been taken off its hinges. The gaping place where the door once stood now announces, "Friend, come in. Here God is spoken about with love." Our hearts must be open to all hearts. It is important to learn this in the pool of silence, because once you open that door, you cannot close it again. You will be hurt, and you will have to face and accept that hurt. We can easily be hurt by strangers. But I don't expect to be hurt by my friends, and this is where great pain can come. People will walk through that open door of your heart, and they will hurt you. You must be ready as Christ was ready. He was hurt physically, mentally and psychologically. At one point he thought that even his Father had abandoned him. He died for us. If he was ready for this, so must we be.

When we are prepared for pain in this way, something very strange happens to us. The pain results in joy! If I am prepared for the possibility that the person who comes through the open door of my heart may hit me, and if I really believe that I belong to God, this moment is a moment of joy. When you are ready for pain, not only does it hurt *you* less, but it has an influence on the other. You may not see its fruits, but they will be present. We must accept the fact that pain is inevitable for the follower of Christ.

The only ideas for which we are permitted to fight

are matters of conscience. Otherwise our ideas must be plunged into the pool of silence. I don't know what happens there. Is it like using a scrub brush or a detergent? Whatever it is, once your thoughts are plunged into that vast pool, you begin thinking before you speak — but you don't think with your head. You begin to think with your heart, and everything changes.

Do we want to open our hearts? Do we want to open them to pain, to joy, to everything? Our motive must be charity, because that is God's motive. If that is our motivation, and if we truly open our hearts, then we will automatically think alike in matters of the Spirit. *Sobornost*, oneness in the Spirit, will be ours. You have opened your heart, I have opened mine, and we have gone together into the pool of silence where we know God is present. Now we begin to use words carefully, almost haltingly, and our words become different. As our words change, the doors of our heart open still wider. As they open, people enter. We begin to know each other, and we become one in the great pool of silence.

PRAYER: A Soul's Question

Into the strange, awesome glory of your face, you drew my soul.

In that immense, immeasurable power, I am a nothing that reflects your light. The weight of the light would bring me death. But you pour into it your life.

O Lord of hosts, of might and glory, O uncreated, infinite One! What traffic have you with dust? Do you rejoice in seeing a speck of dust dance in your light? Or, incredibly, does your mercy deign to fill this speck of dust with your own life?

Into the strange, awesome glory of your face, you drew my soul.

16

WHEN YOU GO TO THE POUSTINIA

Many people all over the world have read my book *Poustinia*, but there is so much misunderstanding as to what the experience of the poustinia really is that I wilt a little when I think about it!

First and foremost, when you go to the poustinia, *don't worry about prayer.* You take one book with you: the scriptures. Don't get all anxious, saying, "I've got to pray, I've got to pray. How do I do it? What do the scriptures say to do?" No. You walk in, bless yourself, bow to the crucifix or icon, and say to yourself, "Peace be to this house and to me." That's all you have to do.

If you're tired, sleep. Have a good sleep, and you'll feel better afterward. You may sleep for 24 hours, but you will be praying while you do so: "I sleep but my heart watches." Perhaps you take a walk. It doesn't matter whether you're in the country or in the city. Be completely natural. Prayer is rest. Breathe in the breath of the Spirit. Be free. Be simple. Prayer is a perfectly natural relationship between God, who loved you first, and you who try to love him back.

The other day I received a letter from a woman who wrote, "I went into the poustinia, and I could barely wait for it to end because my head was whirring so." She said she couldn't pray because her head was buzzing with a multitude of concerns and activities. This woman had a totally false conception of prayer.

The soul's entry into the poustinia should be totally relaxed. Maybe you're too neurotic to relax at first! In that case, let the poustinia itself relax you. There's nothing to get excited about. Unless you settle down and find peace in the poustinia, you'll never be able to reach the union with God that you seek there.

So, if you want a cup of coffee or tea, go right ahead. Drink 20 cups if you want! Divide your bread into three sections for breakfast, lunch and dinner, or if you prefer, eat it all at once. There has to be a sense of freedom and simplicity about these things.

In the poustinia, there is absolutely no structure. Why do you have to look for structures when you come there? When people go to the poustinia, their first question is always, "What do I do?" Well, what would you do in a real desert, alone with no one to talk to, and only the scriptures at hand? Well, do that in the poustinia, and be free about it. Be utterly, completely free. Be free from anything that would distract you. You are outside the normal restrictions of time, and you can do what you jolly well please!

You have come to the poustinia to pray. Now, what does that mean? There is the prayer of petition. Of course it's good to pray for everyone, but the Lord knows himself what everyone needs. Leave your lists of petitions outside, and say to him simply, "Lord, you know I come with all the needs of all the people who want me to pray for them, but for once, I am simply going to give them to you and let you take care of them all." That ends the conversation.

You're going to meditate. What is that all about? It's as if you had a boyfriend or girlfriend and you sit thinking nice things about him or her. In other words, you think about the person you're really interested in. The person who really interests you is God. So you think about him. You think about his words, which you can read in the scriptures.

But there is something else. There is contemplation. Contemplation means to look at someone in silence, and this is where the poustinia comes in. You enter the poustinia in the silence of a heart which has ceased to worry about anything and is completely open to the other.

Whether you are looking at the trees as you walk, or looking at the people on the city streets, or just sitting in your little room, the face of Christ is before you, and you know that your face is before him. You are lost in the heart of him who loves you and whom you love. That is all. That is the poustinia.

A bride instinctively throws herself into the arms of her bridegroom. She doesn't say to herself when he comes home, "Now, what am I doing to do? Shall I throw myself into his left arm or his right arm?" When you go to God in the poustinia, just put your head in your heart and really see him. Be simple, be like a child, and have fun with God. There are no structures, and no one can tell you to do this or that.

Do not confuse the poustinia with a house of prayer. In the poustinia, one person lives apart from everyone else. It may be a room in a house with others, but when you enter the poustinia, you are alone.

Another unusual aspect of the poustinia is that you

don't go to Mass during that time. The Mass comes to you, in the sense that God comes to you in a very special way. You enter into this contemplation, and the poustinia brings you to silence, the silence of the desert, the immense silence where your heart meets the heart of God.

You continue in this silence until you reach the Absolute. It might take a long time or it might not, but in the process, you will become a prayer. You are not praying with your lips, nor with your head. You are not even praying with your heart. As St. John of the Cross wrote in one of his poems, "At night, when all the house was quiet, I left without anyone knowing and went to a rendezvous with my God." In this state, all senses are suspended. When that happens to you, you will have become a prayer, and eventually you will reach the Absolute. This is the essence of the poustinia.

To go to the poustinia is simply to rest one's head on the breast of God, listening to his heartbeats. It is imposssible to grasp this with the mind. You will understand it only with your heart — a heart that is in touch with the heart of God.

PRAYER: Let My Heart Repose

O Lord of peace, keep me within your heart. Let me rest upon your breast, no matter where I am.

My feet may fly upon a thousand tasks for you, my hands be busy with things to do for you, my mind immersed in thoughts and plans for you. But let my heart repose within your heart, for then I will be truly blessed by you.

I hunger so for that repose in you. My heart is restless unless it rests in you.

As time flies by, my heart hungers more and more for silence, for solitude. I am so parched for both, it is like walking in a burning desert to be without them.

Oh, grant me the grace of silence, solitude of heart amid the milling, noisy throngs who fill my days. Oh, grant me repose and rest within your heart amid ceaseless activity on your behalf.

O Lover, come, take possession of my heart, and keep it forever within your Sacred Heart.

17

PRAYER AND SOLITUDE

Prayer is "in"! So is solitude. Everywhere, people are talking about houses of prayer. Everyone wants to run away to a prayer house or hermitage. Everyone wants to go live somewhere far away from everything and pray. Why is this?

Are they running from what is in fact an intolerable situation, that of modern urban living? Or is this just another way of escaping from what irks us? If the latter, we will soon discover that what bothers us ultimately is ourselves—the one thing we can't leave behind when we go into solitude.

On the other hand, could it be that the voice of God is truly calling this person or that person to a certain kind of prayer? How do I know the difference? How do I know if it is my will or the will of the Father? It could so easily be my own will.

Many prayer houses have been born, but have died in their infancy. Some have started, but are barely able to keep going. Others have ended tragically in quarrels and difficulties. Why? I don't know the answer. I do know that a prayer house or a hermitage without love and peace is not a place of prayer.

Why is there this wave of prayer houses? You might say to me, "Just look at the evil all around." But my next question will be, "If I am a Christian, should I run from evil or should I enter the ring and fight it?" The real question is, *How* should I fight evil? By living in a poustinia? By living in a ghetto? By staying in the city? By remaining right where I am?

Our prayer must be upheld by our life. I can spend my whole day praying. I can be a mystic of the first order. I might even levitate or have the stigmata. But the test is always, "By their fruits you shall know them." Prayer can change things only if *I* change with my prayer. Then prayer will and must bear fruit, fruit which is acceptable to God.

That is why it is wrong when people speak of prayer houses and poustinias as if this were the only way to pray. No, no, no! First you must make a house of prayer in your own heart. Begin with that. Stand still. Find God in yourself, on your journey inward. Interiorize your poustinia, your house of prayer, in order to find out if God is really calling you to a life of solitude.

It is very important to differentiate between prayer and solitude. Prayer is the fundamental act of the Christian, his very life. Prayer is continuous in a heart that loves, and it doesn't need solitude any more than joy needs solitude. When you are in love with someone and you get engaged, of course you want to be alone with your fiance, but you still have to keep on working. As I have said so often, you can make love everywhere, because lovemaking is not only performing the marriage act. Lovemaking can be two people holding hands in a special way. Lovemaking can be two people not even touching each other, but deeply aware of each other's presence.

Prayer is contact with God such as lovers have, such as friends have. It doesn't need solitude to exist. Occasionally it is nice to have it but let's not make the mistake of thinking that we can only pray to God if we can get away from the mob and escape to the solitude of a Russian-style poustinia. We have to be realistic about prayer. Prayer is, first and foremost, standing still before God. Before you even begin to ask questions about prayer, you must stand still.

But of course I am pursued by questions! But how can anyone tell you about prayer? Only God can explain it. You can read about it in a book. You can ask someone who is prayerful and he or she will tell you something about it. But the essence of prayer cannot be communicated. None of us can be an expert on prayer. St. Teresa of Avila wrote her books under obedience to her spiritual director, but there are no words to express those kinds of experiences. When you read her books and those of St. John of the Cross, and all the great mystics, you kind of get left behind. Speaking for myself, I read them and I say, "Well, this is beautiful — but what about me?"

No one can teach us to pray except God. How can I tell you what happened to me and my husband on our wedding night? What has been said and done remains our secret. When our lover is God, prayer is a secret between the king and the one he has chosen for his bride.

Prayer is something like a continuous wedding night. It is stillness. It is lovemaking. Who can describe how God makes love to us and how we make love to

God? Who can tell you how to stand still before the miracle of love? Who can describe how one cries out with joy because Christ is a human being who runs with us, plays with us, befriends us, drinks a cup of coffee with us! How are you going to explain all this? You have to remain still and wait. God himself will come and tell you about it.

Once all this has been interiorized over a long period of time, then perhaps God will call you to solitude. Solitude is a very special vocation. It is God saying, "Come with me into the desert and pray all day and all night. I want you to be in solitude so that you might walk among men in the dark of their night, with quiet feet."

If solitude is not your vocation, and you have confused it with prayer, you may go off to be alone and then find that you can't pray at all, that the fruits do not justify your staying there. Be careful, now that you are disenchanted with solitude, that you do not leave behind prayer as well!

It is true that there is a special loneliness which is part of the vocation to solitude. But loneliness is also part of the ordinary Christian vocation, simply because loneliness is part of silence. In order to really pray, you need that strange silence to surround your prayer and allow it to come forth. This silence is not an outward reality but an inner one, and this is what all of us have so much difficulty understanding. I don't need solitude to pray, but I do need inner silence. Then I can pray any time. I can even pray as I talk to you.

I agree with the idea that it helps to have an environment that generates peace. This has always been the Benedictine ideal. But that environment does not have to be a monastery. It can be a family or community that is in love with God, and which therefore creates an environment where people can find the inner silence they need. Whether it be a blood family, a parish community, a university group, or whatever, the important thing is that the members love one another. The important thing is that they love their enemies (parents, superiors, "the establishment"). When we love, the criticisms we make will not be vindictive. But if we fail to love, we will be out of touch with Christ, and our prayer life will be fruitless indeed.

PRAYER: Loneliness

What strange mystery is this, O Christ?
The closer I approach your love, the lonelier I
become.

It seems as if, indeed, it is *terribilis* to fall
into the hands of the loving God. Alone, the
shadow of your face crushes my heart and
brings about a host of fears.

Your weight is so immense; the world
seems weightless against your weight. And
loneliness complete seems to embrace me,
severing all ties with human beings, yet not
binding me to you.

Tremendous Lover, is this your way to
bring a soul into your courts, where she can
wash herself in tears and be bedecked in the
heavy mantle of loneliness beyond any known
on earth, so that she understands that
loneliness is fire of desire for you, the Desired
One?

18

THE LAND OF LONELINESS

Where does the life of prayer lead? Toward the end of the journey inward, after one has met Christ and shared his cross, one enters a strange land of loneliness. Peace seems to precede it. It think it is the peace that comes through having been crucified. There is a moment of resurrection, as if one has been taken off the cross. The wounds are not healed, but they no longer hurt.

You are different. You are different because now you know that God exists, and he alone matters. It is an overwhelming, awesome thought. It could be an annihilating thought, had you not in some way shared in his crucifixion yourself. You are different in the sense that now all people belong to you and are part of you, and you belong to all people. At the same time, you belong only to God, and you belong to him totally. There is a distinction between you and others, and at the same time, there is no distinction at all, but a blending of all into one. The demarcation that exists is a spiritual

125

one, born of what you have lived and what you can never explain. This is the land of loneliness.

There are no words for this. The land of loneliness is the land of joy. It is the land of union with God. The land of loneliness is the land of hunger for God. The land of loneliness is one of belonging to God and understanding that God alone matters.

The secret of this land is that the hunger for God grows in you like fire. In fact, it *is* fire. At the same time, the love of humanity is intensified. There is only one thought in the land of loneliness, one dream, one passion,one desire: to lead people to God.

But people do not want to go to God! This is the loneliness that Christ experienced throughout his whole life, most intensely in the garden of Gethsemane. In the land of loneliness one knows, perhaps only a little but with intense passion, who God is. You desire with a passionate desire to give him to every man, woman and child. Then you discover that people do not want to accept him. They will give him a token of themselves, a part of themselves, but they do not want to give all of themselves to God.

So you walk in the land of loneliness. In that land, there is no possibility of manipulating others. You can't do it because God will not allow it. It is he who is in charge, not you. He who walks in the land of loneliness is on the way to saying, "I live now, not I, but Christ lives in me." Not that we all aren't still sinners; not that the weight of God doesn't continue to lie heavily upon us. But the call remains to lead all people to God.

To enter the land of loneliness, all my needs must be directed toward God alone. Many of the needs are still there; they have not disappeared. They constitute my tunic, the only tunic worn by the pilgrim in the land of loneliness. Sometimes the tunic seems like a hairshirt; at other times, it is soft and downy. It symbolizes something I have come to understand a little: the fact that we tend to need each other differently from the way in which God wants us to need each other. One of the fruits of this strange journey is that those who enter the land of loneliness are received back by Christ, and they receive everyone back in him.

The need for approval, the need to say everything in our mind, the need to be needed, the need to direct others toward myself, to impress them by my intellect, my capabilities — these needs all fall away. In the land of loneliness, friendship becomes simple and joyous. Because all needs are centered in Christ, my own insignificance no longer matters to me. The one flaming desire to bring all people to God seems to soften the impact of all these things. The human heart, as far as it is able, now opens itself to total possession by God. Now one understands, in the light of this incredible reality that without him we can do nothing.

You are reduced at first to a state of seeming nonbeing. The wings of the intellect fold, the heart opens, and the intellect is illuminated by Christ. Now one understands a little more fully the words of St. Teresa of Avila that "I and a ducat are nothing, but I, a ducat, and God, are everything." To paraphrase her statement: "I cannot lead anyone anywhere by myself, but if I allow myself to be filled with God, I can lead all to God."

The road which began at baptism and continued with the Eucharist, confirmation and contemplation of the Beloved has finally led me through the passion and the cross, and brought me to the land of loneliness. It is a land of strange peace and intense joy, but it is a land of loneliness. I think it is the last step before total union with God. For some of us, many perhaps, this union may come before our death—if we love enough, if our heart is open enough, and if God desires it so.

PRAYER: A Seed

I was a seed of wheat. You were the sower. You buried me in the deep, dark furrow one day so long ago. I died a thousand deaths within that earth so dark, so rich, so warm, so cold, and yet I lived.

Twice I believed that it was time to bring forth fruit. But twice the storms of hatred, of scorn, froze the furrow and the earth.

Then, when it seemed to me I died my thousandth death, the rain, the sun came. And beneath its warm rays I brought forth my seeds and laid them in your hands to die again and multiply. Amen.